BOOTS ON THE GROUND

Bruce McEwen

A 21 Day devotional to inspire and encourage the warrior within you, to awaken and be who you are called to be in Jesus.

Day 1. The Call.

2 Timothy 2:3(ESV)

Share in the suffering as a good soldier of Christ Jesus.

As a former infantry soldier, I know only too well the suffering a soldier goes though. Lack of sleep, cold, wet, hungry on a regular basis. Exhausted, carrying heavy loads, working in extreme temperatures, dangerous environments, yet ready to take the fight to the enemy. It all went with the job, what made a soldier stand out from a civilian is a soldier expects and is prepared to suffer. To lay down his life for his fellow soldier, prepared to fight for and defend the freedom of others.

In the scripture Paul is writing to his young friend Timothy to encourage and commission him. Paul is telling Timothy in the letter to keep pushing on to answer the call and to be prepared to suffer as a Soldier of Jesus. To not to be taken by surprise what will come against him and suffering for Jesus will come with the territory.

Today as you read this first devotional, Jesus is encouraging you to answer the call. For the warrior in you to awaken and to prepare for spiritual battle. Step up and step out as a soldier of Jesus Christ and fight the good fight of faith. Be bold be courageous and share Jesus with anyone willing to listen. Be prepared to suffer but know this Jesus is with you, His promise is He will never leave you nor forsake you. He is with you each step of the way on this 21 Day journey and beyond.

Day 2. Come unto Me.

Matthew 11:28-30(ESV)

Come to me, all who labour and are heavy laden, and I will give you rest. Take my yoke upon you, and learn from me, for I am gentle and lowly in heart, and you will find rest for your souls. For My yoke is easy and My burden is light.

Years ago, I went through an emotional and mental breakdown. For too long I was trying to hold it all together and do everything in my own strength. The stress of serving in a war zone, dealing with the loss of a child, a marriage breakdown. In denial about alcohol addiction, trying to keep my inner demons at bay and depression knocking at my door. I was meant to be tough soldier, a war veteran, a leader of men. Weakness was not an option, but then it happened! I broke down and was at the end of myself. I couldn't function, I was overwhelmed, I lost all hope. I tried to take my own life. I battled like this for years after until when I wasn't even looking for Him, Jesus showed up and changed everything.

You too may be at the end of yourself and totally broken. You may be looking to end your life. Please don't, know this, Jesus is holding out His scarred hands to you right now and saying "Come to me." Jesus will take your pain, your mess and your struggles, He will give you His Peace, His Joy, Jesus will walk with you each step you take, right by your side. In Him we can walk in Victory. Give everything you're carrying to Jesus and allow Him to work in your life. He will never turn anyone away who comes to Him.

Day 3. Know who you are.

1 John 4:4(ESV)

Little children, you are from God and have overcome them, for He who is in you is greater than he who is in the world.

As a soldier I knew who I was and what I was capable of. It was my very identity and this in turn impacted my skills and capabilities and enabled me to serve efficiently and effectively under extreme conditions in a war zone. I didn't need to worry about myself as I knew my mates had my back and I had there's. Whatever situation we found ourselves in no one would ever be left behind. We were soldiers and young. This was our identity and we knew who we were.

John is writing in this letter to fellow believers to remember just Who it is that's in them. To stand on their identity as a child of God because in doing so no matter what the world throws at them, they can stand firm and stand strong because of Who it is that has their backs.

As a child of God if you would truly know Who is it is that's in you and Who is behind you, then there is nothing that can come against you that will break you or overwhelm you. Its in Jesus we can and will walk in Victory, even when it feels like the world is falling apart all around us. We can still be at peace knowing Jesus has got our back.

Day 4. You are not forsaken.

Hebrews 13:5(ESV)

I will never leave you nor forsake you.

John 6:37(ESV)

And whoever comes to me I will never cast out.

After my complete breakdown and trying to take my own life I truly experienced being rejected and alienated by some of the very guys I served with and went to war with. I was treated as an outcast by many of my fellow soldiers. I felt shame, guilt rejection and so many other emotions. Even eventually forsaken by the very Regiment I gave my everything to, deemed no longer fit for service or needed. I know only too well what it feels to be alone, a social outcast with no value and no hope. But that all changed When Jesus showed up and loved me when I was at my most unlovable.

Over three times it is written in the Word where Jesus promises He will never leave you nor forsake you. Even in the Gospel of John Jesus declares His promise He will never turn anyone away that comes to Him.

I don't know where you at today but wherever you are and however you feeling know that Jesus is for you, He loves you, even at your most unlovable state. You are so precious to Him that He even gave His life for you so you could be redeemed and accepted unto Him as His Child. Today reach out to Him and let Him embrace you,

Day 5. Boots On The Ground.

Joshua 1:3(ESV)

Every place that the sole of your foot will tread upon I have given you

As an infantry soldier one of our key elements was to dominate and deny the enemy ground. This could only be done by having boots on the ground and taking the fight to the enemy if needs be.

In Joshua chapter 1 The LORD is commissioning and preparing Joshua to take the land that He promised the Israelites. He is encouraging Joshua that He will give Him the ground He treads upon and nothing will stop him that comes against Him. Joshua is receiving his battle orders.

Today Jesus promises you the same thing. He is giving you your battle orders. Jesus will give you the ground you tread upon. He is commanding and encouraging you to take the Gospel with you. To share Jesus with anyone willing to listen, whether that is you home with your family, your workplace or your social settings with friends. Know that the ground has been given to you. Be bold and courageous and get those Boots on the Ground, for nothing can overcome you or overwhelm you. Because you Have Jesus in you with you and Behind you. Be the Light wherever you go and the darker the place the brighter you will shine.

Day 6. Stand firm.

2 Chronicles 20:17(ESV)

You will not need to fight in this battle. Stand firm, hold your position, and see the salvation of the Lord on your behalf, O Judah and Jerusalem. Do not be afraid and do not be dismayed. Tomorrow go out against them and the LORD will be with you.

I remember all too well all the intensive public order training I did with my Squadron and the R.U.C in Northern Ireland. We would stand firm and hold our position as the rioters would taunt us and throw abuse and stones and petrol bombs at us. At a moment's notice if the situation escalates, we would respond with swift and appropriate action.

Here God is commanding Jehoshaphat to stand firm, hold his position and watch the Lord fight on his behalf. But to go out again and again and watch how the Lord will deliver his enemies into his hands. That God is always with Him.

That is Jesus's command to you today, to stand firm and hold your position in that pick your battles carefully. You don't need to fight every single one every single time. The Lord will vindicate you when your badly treated, someone speaks of you and slanders you or you find yourself in an unjust situation. All He is asking is to live it out each day, walk the walk, continue to love and forgive others no matter what, to continue to show grace and mercy. For the Lord is with you each step fighting the battles for you.

Day 7. Leave no one behind.

Luke 15:4(ESV)

What man of you having a hundred sheep, if he has lost one of them, does not leave the ninety-nine in the open country, and go after the one that is lost, until he finds it.

On the build up to the Iraq War one of the most crucial drills we practised over and over was casualty evacuation drills if we came under fire from the enemy. The reason being for being so meticulous, was we would never leave anyone behind in a firefight.

In the Luke 15 Jesus is using a parable to explain that just one soul is precious to Him that He will deliberately go after that one person who is so lost, has lost all hope and is even at the end of themselves. He uses the example of a sheep because we can be like sheep that we just wonder off blindly down a path not considering the choices we make and the consequences of them.

I believe Jesus is encouraging us today to be like the shepherd and go after that one lost sheep, to get out of our comfort zone and reach out to that one person who is in pain, who is broken, struggling with addiction, or depression or even suicide. Just love them where they are at with the love of Jesus. For me this is a life scripture because Jesus came after me when I was so lost. That is why I go after one person at a time to love them like Jesus and show them they are not alone. Don't leave anyone behind warriors.

Day 8. Snatch them from danger.

Jude 22,23(ESV)

And have mercy on those who doubt: save others by snatching them out of the fire; to other show mercy with fear, hating even the garment stained by the flesh.

When we invaded Iraq were expectant of a fight. Yet that fight never initially came we remained prepared for one. Meanwhile we showed respect, compassion and mercy to the local civilians, even helping them wherever we could. We also warned them of the dangers of getting in the way of the impeding coalition forces as war was moving through their nation.

Jude is writing to believers to equip and encourage them to show mercy to those who even hated them, to warn them of the coming danger. Importantly to stand out and stand apart from those who lived differently to what God commands. But all importantly to show respect, compassion, mercy and to be gentle regardless of how they themselves were treated.

As believers Jesus is asking us to always be gentle with others and how we interact and share the Gospel with them. To always be respectful regardless of what they believe or how they live their lives. If given an opportunity to share in love but with a boldness, the urgency of the days we are living. That Jesus is the ONLY WAY to God. Like a fireman who would run into a building to pull someone from a fire, we need to share the reality of hell. A taboo subject but the reality many are heading there and we need to snatch them from the flames. Regardless of what others may say or think, always show respect and be gentle my fellow warriors.

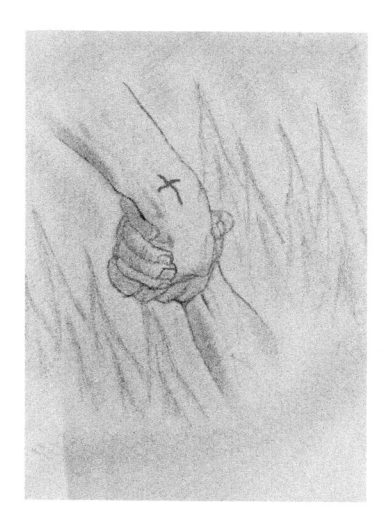

Day 9. You are a new creation.

2 Corinthians 5:17(ESV)

Therefore, if anyone is in Christ, he is a new creation. The old has past away; behold, the new, has come.

When I was at the height of my bodybuilding days, I would look at myself in the mirror and never be satisfied with the physique looking back. Wanting to be bigger here or slimmer there, striving to gain the perfect physique but never attaining my goal. When I had my complete breakdown, looking in the mirror the night I tried to take my own life, I hated who was looking back at me.

In Corinthians Paul is writing to the church at Corinth, explaining that if indeed they have given everything to Christ, they are not who they were. They are a brand-new person (born again as the term goes). Their old life is gone, so why go back to old patterns of behaviour, old habits, old ways of living. To look forward to what Jesus has for them. To stand on the assurance Jesus is in them and with them, to keep walking forward and not look back.

When you look in the mirror what do you see? If you are a follower of Jesus then stop seeing the old you because that is not you. People will be quick to say you have not changed, you're still the same. Especially point out your flaws and faults. When we come to Jesus, yes, we are transformed into His children but we are miraculously perfect. We still have struggles, hurts and hang ups even maybe addictions and other baggage. People will be quick to try and pull you down. But look to Jesus and allow Him to work in your life. Know your identity warriors. You are a child of God. In Him you can and will walk in victory.

Day 10. I Stand at the door and knock.

Revelation 3:20(ESV)
Behold I stand at the door and knock. If anyone hears my voice and opens the door, I will come in to him and eat with him, and he with Me.

With Covid Lockdown in full swing these days like many I'm sure, I miss friends and family coming round knocking on the door and inviting them in and having a great time with them. The only knocks I get at the door these days is the Amazon man delivering my parcels from things I have ordered.

In Revelation Jesus is speaking to John and explaining to him that He knocks on the door of everyone's heart waiting patiently for them to answer. That if anyone would open their heart to Him and give their life to Him, He will be in them and with them for all eternity. Jesus is a gentleman He will never force Himself into anyone's life. He certainly won't kick the door in like a police search and entry team. Jesus invites everyone to come to Him, that's right everyone.

Where are you at today in your own life fellow warrior? Are there aspects of your life or your heart you have closed of today to Jesus? Have you or are you hardening your heart towards Jesus? Do you feel you lukewarm in your walk with Him, even grown cold towards Him? Wherever you're at today I want to encourage you Jesus is still with you, He is still knocking at the door of your Heart to invite Him in again. He is still waiting with open arms to embrace you. There is nothing you can do that will make Him forsake you or not forgive you. Just turn to Him and open your heart to Him and He will stir up that fire within you again. Jesus has not forgotten you and He will never leave you. For those that don't know Him, He too is knocking at the door of your heart and asking you with all His love. Will you let Me in?

Day 11. God sees the heart.

1 Samuel 16:7(ESV)
But the LORD said to Samuel, "Do not look on his appearance or on the height of his stature, because I have rejected him. For the LORD sees not the outward appearance: but the LORD looks on the heart.

In my bodybuilding days I prided myself on having a powerful physique and looking like someone not to be messed with. For a long time I tried to be the tough man not allowing anyone to take advantage or get one over me. But inside I was a broken mess, that was hurting, had no hope and yearned for longing and acceptance.

Here God is saying to Samuel to reject David's brothers who were likely big strong men and the ideal choice in mans eyes. Samuel weas to anoint David even though he was just a shepherd boy, for God knew David's heart and how it was right before God.

Sadly society is impressed with appearance and one's own strength and ability, but God is not. What is truly important to God is the condition of our heart which should be gentle, humble and teachable. Surrender your heart today before God and allow these qualities to shine through and God will delight in using you mightily for His Glory.

Day 12. Walk the walk.

Isaiah 52:7(ESV)
How beautiful upon the mountains are the feet of Him who brings the good news.

As a former soldier our feet were our most important mode of transport. I have lost count the amount of hours and days going out on foot patrol carrying a rifle and heavy equipment, exhausted and lack of sleep. I have patrolled the streets of West Belfast to the arid desert of Iraq and yet my trusted feet and issued boots have carried me through.

The drawing is one of my most favourite I have done. It depicts Jesus having just been baptised, walking into the wilderness and the journey begins of Him bringing salvation to all and His plan of redemption set in motion.

Today warriors it's important we are Jesus's foot soldiers. That we be the boots on the ground walking the walk and letting our lights shine in the darkness. I believe Jesus is encouraging you today to go into every place and continue to share Him with anyone willing to listen. People spot authenticity a mile off so it's important we walk the walk and not just talk the talk.

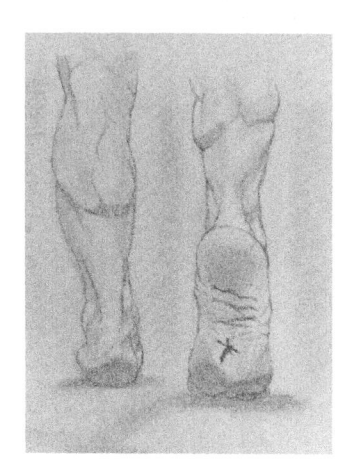

Day 13. Always be gentle and show respect.

1 Peter 3:15(ESV)
But in your hearts honour Christ the Lord as Holy, always being prepared to make a defence to anyone who asks you for a reason for the hope that is in you; yet do it with gentleness and respect.

This is something the Lord has been speaking to me personally on for some time. He has been showing me how important it is to be respectful to others regardless of their moral choices, lifestyle or even how they identify themselves as. The Lord has given me a gentle heart so this coincides with sharing Jesus with others in a gentle way. There are too many people out there who claim to be believers but speak harshly and critically over others with no true love in doing so.

Peter here is sharing in his letter to other believers to firstly be obedient to the Lord in everything they do, but also always be prepared to speak in boldness and share Jesus and His truth with anyone who would want to listen. But the key is to do it with respect and in a gentle way.

Today fellow warriors its key that we let out light shine brightly and be ready to share Jesus with anyone who asks what is it that we have. Always be respectful and love others where they are at regardless. But always be gentle. Acceptance does not mean agreement. We can share in love the truth and not water down the truth and still be loving regardless of differences.

Day 14. The Watchman.

Ezekiel 3:17(ESV)
"Son of man, I have made you a watchman for the house of Israel. Whenever you hear a Word from My mouth, you shall give them warning from Me."

When serving in Iraq one role I would have to frequently carry out is Sentry on the main gate at Basrah Airport. In an elevated protective sangar with a heavy machine gun, I would be the eyes and ears and first line of defence for anyone who fancied their chances of coming onto the base uninvited.

Ezekiel was commissioned to be a watchman for Israel, to also prophesy of this calling upon people, even for people today. The role of the watchman in Israel was to man a watchtower while the city slept. It was the watchman's job to bring warning of any impeding attack, to wake up the city and be ready. That role today spiritually is for leaders to keep watch and bring warning to the body of believers what is coming.

All of us in the body of Christ in some-way are called to be watchman to bring warning of what is coming and the return of Jesus. Some believers are specifically called into this role to share specifically of what is coming on this world and the days we are living in. We can only do this by keeping our eyes on Jesus, spending time with Him and in His Word. Then He will reveal to us what He wants us to share with others. Warriors stay alert keep your eyes on Jesus.

Day 15. Are you a foot washer or a stone thrower.

John 13:5(ESV)
Then He poured water into a basin and began to wash the disciples' feet and to wipe them with the towel wrapped around Him.

"If you knew you only had one day to live, what would you do with your time? Jesus did and He washed the feet of the very man that would betray Him to His death!)

One of the greatest scenes in the Bible is Jesus the Son of God, the King of Kings and Lord of lords humbling Himself and getting down and washing the feet of His own disciples. Jesus knew exactly what He was doing and was setting the example of true humility He wants in all His followers. He showed unbelievable love, compassion, grace, mercy and forgiveness in that He washed the feet of Judas Iscariot, the very man that would betray Him to His own death. Jesus set the stage so we are without excuse in how we treat others.

It's all to easy to forget where we have come from and judge and criticise others when they are not living according to what we expect people should. It's then we become the stone throwers like the religious zealots of Jesus's day. So I want to encourage you today to look to this scene and remember what Jesus did as a sign of humility. Regardless of how someone treats you or speaks against you show humility, grace, mercy, compassion and love. Choose to forgive no matter what. Ask yourself one question. "Am I a foot washer or a stone thrower?"

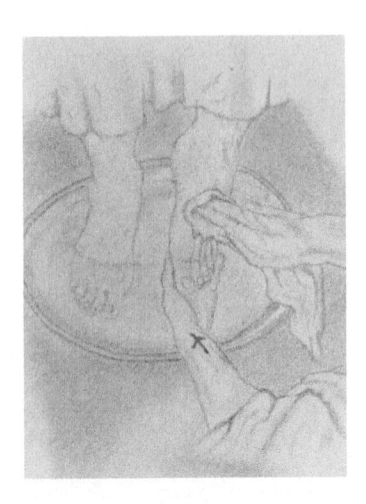

Day 16. Always be ready.

Matthew 22:44(ESV)
Therefore you also must be ready, for the Son of Man is coming at an hour you do not expect.

There is coming a day when God will say "Enough." He will Look to Jesus and say "Now!" Jesus will stand up take one step forward and the whole world will see Him. As the saying goes the Lion is about to roar and everyone will see Him.

One of my favourite scenes from 'The Lion the Witch and the wardrobe' is when they seemed defeated and all hope is gone, they believe Aslan is dead and then He appears in all His Glory and gives a mighty roar. Everyone rejoices. I believe this depicts an analogy of when Jesus returns and many will rejoice but yet many will be caught unaware, devastated and realise its too late.

We are living in urgent times and don't have time to waste, we can't afford to be wasting time and be asleep and go through the motions. Jesus's return is imminent, that is why we need to be ready. So today warriors, let's wake ourselves up and be ready. Keep short accounts with God, walk in humility, continue to forgive, show grace and mercy to others. Remember where we have come from and share Jesus with the lost and broken of this world. Be the light and be authentic. We need to stop living like the world and be set apart. For the Lion is about to Roar.

Day 17. It's never too late.

Judges 16:28(ESV)
Then Samson called to the LORD and said "O Lord GOD, please remember me and please strengthen me only this once, O God, that I may be avenged on the philistines for my two eyes."

Samson was anointed to great things for God and given mighty strength to Judge Israel and lead them. Sadly he wasted his anointing and his calling, he was distracted by his own lustful wants and needs which led to his demise and tragic yet brutal capture torture and humiliation. Samson had chance after chance but he blew it. In his biggest humiliation he humbled himself and cried out to God for mercy. God showed great compassion and forgiveness to Samson and in his last moments God used him greater than in all the things he had done for God combined previously.

You may have blown it yourself. You may feel God will now never use me. You may feel all hope is gone and its too late. Be encouraged it's never too late, you can never blow it enough for God to use you again. If you have blown it as we all do at some point, now is the time to humble yourself and call out to God for mercy. Run to Him not from Him, repent of what you have done and |I truly believe God will use you mightier than He has ever done before.

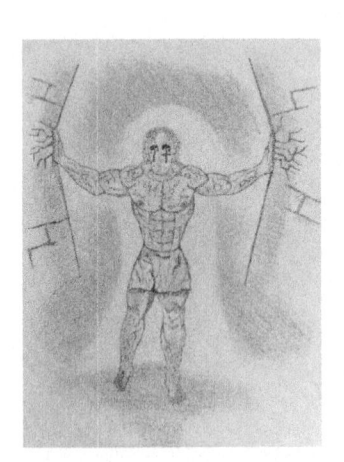

Day 18. Giant slayer.

2 Corinthians 12:10(ESV)
For the sake of Christ, then I am content with weaknesses, insults, hardships, persecutions, and calamities. For when I am weak, then I am strong.

Goliath was a giant a man of war, combat was what he lived and breathed. But yet a shepherd boy was not afraid to go out against him. David wasn't anything special but simply a boy with a surrendered heart to God. He went out against Goliath under the leading and anointing of God. What I love is David ran towards Goliath under the complete trust and strength of God. He slew him with a stone and then cut his head off with his own sword. Declaring "that all the earth will know that there is a God in Israel." (1 Samuel 17:46ESV)

Even Paul boasted of in own his weakness God will show how mighty and strong He is. I don't know what your giant is that is overwhelming you or about to destroy you. But be encouraged embrace your weakness, keep your eyes on Jesus and allow God to lead you into your battle and allow His Word to slay that giant in your life. Stand on the Word of God declare it over your situation, allow God to show how mighty He is and slay that giant. So you can declare to the world and everyone will know and see. "That everyone will know there is a God in Heaven."

Day 19. Walking through the darkest valley.

Psalm 23:4(ESV)
Even though I walk through the valley of the shadow of death, I will fear no evil, For You are with me; Your rod and Your staff they comfort me.

I remember in my darkest hour when I tried to take my own life, God's hand intervened and carried me through, even though I didn't yet know Him. He has carried me through some of my darkest hours even as a believer because He is faithful.

Psalm 23 is probably the most famous psalm of all and David speaks in it of the faithfulness of God being with Him in the darkest moments of his life even when facing death. David speaks of not fearing but trusting that God is with Him.

You maybe facing your darkest hour, you may be in your deepest and darkest moment of your life. You may be overwhelmed, at the end of yourself and given up. All I can say is please don't give up. Trust in Him, He is with you and He will never leave you not forsake you. He will carry you through. Even if you can only see enough light to put one foot forward, keep walking because He will bring you through that valley. Jesus is with you each step of the way.

Day 20. It is finished.

John 19:30(ESV)
When Jesus had received the sour wine, He said, "It is finished," and He bowed His head and gave up His Spirit.

When Jesus spoke His last words on the Cross "It is Finished," it was just that. His plan of redemption was completed, death was beaten, it had lost its sting, a way was made for man to be reconciled back to God. The most important event in all history was finished. As we draw near to the end of this twenty-one day journey it's so important we remember the work of the Cross and why Jesus went to the Cross and hung on it. Bloodied, tortured, humiliated, rejected and alone. For the first time in all of time Jesus was separated from God.

He hung on that Cross and bore the full wrath of God for all sin so that justice was served. Jesus paid the price none of us can pay so that we can be redeemed and forgiven. So that we can become God's children through one Way alone, Jesus. There is no other way. The Cross and what Jesus did on it is the lynchpin of Christianity. Without it there is no Christianity.

That is why today we should reflect on it and also reflect on it everyday. Our salvation cost the very blood and life of God's only Son Christ Jesus. It is all because of Jesus that we are children of God and what He did alone. We can take no credit in any of it. That is why we must preach Christ Crucified to a lost and dying world and generation. Because they need Jesus, His grace and mercy as much as we do. Today be the light and share Jesus with anyone willing to listen, for we or others may not have tomorrow.

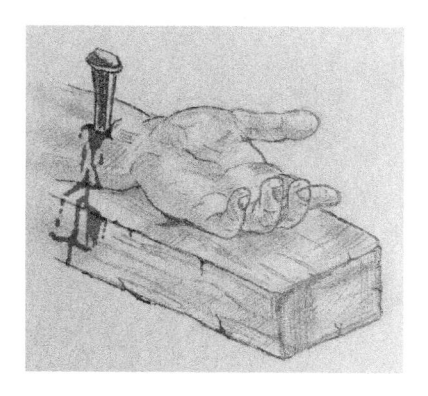

Day 21. First moments in Heaven.

Philippians 3:10(ESV)
That I may know Him and the power of His resurrection, and share in His sufferings, becoming like Him in His death.

Like many others I yearn for the day of Jesus return or If He calls me home, whichever comes first. I yearn to know Him more and more each day. Even when we are in Heaven and been there ten thousand years we will still only know a glimpse of Who He is and His Majesty. Each day is one day closer to His return and we are living in urgent days. We can't afford to waste time, we need to be ready for His return. As this is the last day of this twenty one day journey let us focus on Who He is and His love for each of us. Let us keep our eyes on Him and allow the distractions and the wants of this world to lose its grip on each of us.

Continue to be the light wherever you go, allow His peace to descend upon those around you. Be authentic in everything you do and always be ready to share Jesus with anyone willing to listen. You maybe the only Bible someone will ever read.

I left my favourite drawing till last, I call it 'First Moments in Heaven.' This is how I want to step into eternity and meet my Lord and Saviour Jesus Christ.

Artwork.

All the artwork has been drawn by myself with the inspiration and leading of the Lord Himself. It is the Lord that has given me the gift to be able to draw and a gift I have neglected for so long. My heart is to now use it for His glory. If you would like any copies of the artwork I have done in this book or would like me to draw something particular for you, then you can contact me at the following email and I would be happy to discuss with you what you are looking for in a drawing.

mcewenbruce@yahoo.co.uk

INTO THE WILDERNESS
(The Journey Begins)

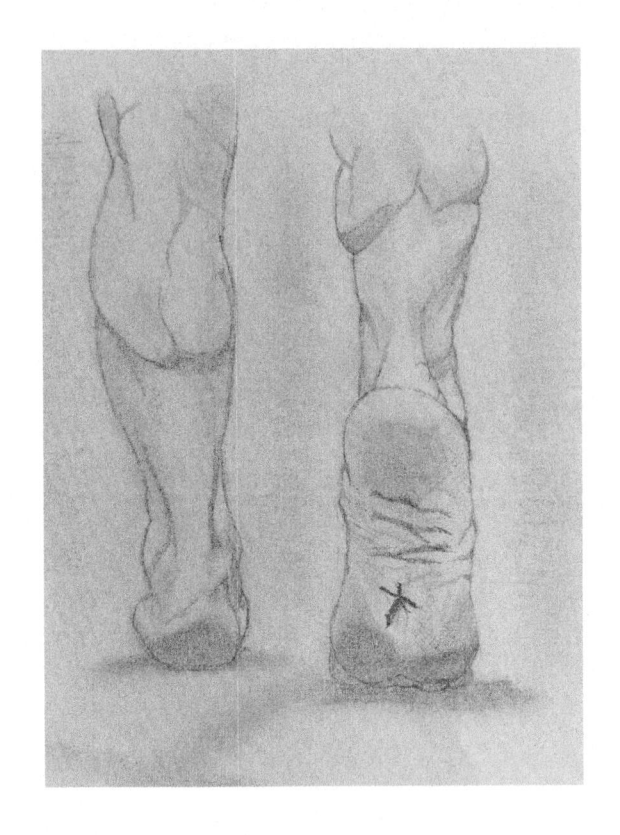

AWAKEN WARRIOR
AND BE THE
BOOTS ON THE GROUND

Printed in Great Britain
by Amazon